The Land of Miracles

By Rev. Nathan M. Meyer, Th.M.

Copyright 1973
BMH Books
Winona Lake, Indiana

Printed in USA

PHOTO CREDITS

The Matson Photo Service
1428 South Marengo
Alhambra, California

Homer A. Kent, Jr.
Winona Lake, Indiana

Levant Photo and Design Service
P.O. Box 1284
Santa Cruz, California

United Press International
New York, New York

TO MARY

who has willingly borne the
cross of being the wife of
an itinerant preacher.

Foreword

BMH Books is very happy to present this book by Nathan Meyer, well-known evangelist and Bible prophecy conference speaker. It contains a sermon that Mr. Meyer has preached on four continents.

On one of Nathan Meyer's many visits to Israel he met Mrs. David Ben Gurion by what appeared to be a chance circumstance. It was God at work though because this introduction later led to the opportunity of meeting the Prime Minister. The discussion between the two men forms the background for the message — the miracles of the new nation, Israel.

To the many who have heard the sermon and to those who have not, this book will prove to be a blessing. It will also serve as a reminder that the Word of God is completely reliable. When God speaks, the results will be what He has declared.

Charles W. Turner
Editor, BMH Books

Table of Contents

Foreword 5

Introduction 9

The Land of Miracles 11

Encounter With Mrs. Ben Gurion 14

First Miracle:
   Preservation of the Jewish People 18

Second Miracle:
   Restoration of the Jewish People 26

Third Miracle:
   Resurrection of a Dead Nation 28

Fourth Miracle:
   Preservation of the New Nation 36

Fifth Miracle:
   Resurrection of a Dead Language 42

Sixth Miracle:
   Restoration of Jerusalem to the Jews . . 42

Restatement of the Miracles 44

Personal Preparation 48

Introduction

Of all prophetic subjects none so stirs the hearts of people in our day as the prophecies pertaining to Israel, the land of miracles. Perhaps that is why I have been requested to deliver the message contained in this booklet more often than any other sermon I have ever preached.

I call it my four thousand dollar sermon because that is exactly what it is. Back in the days of the depression when I was teaching school for eight hundred dollars a year, I never dreamed that God would call me to be a preacher and that on a certain day, after preaching for one hour, He would drop a four thousand dollar gift in my lap.

By the grace of God and in the power of the Holy Spirit, I delivered this message on one occasion some years ago during a blizzard which produced what the government declared to be a "disaster area." It was no disaster for me.

In the audience was a surgeon whom I had never met. His devoted and godly wife had prayed for his spiritual welfare for thirteen years. When I gave the invitation, the doctor walked down the aisle in rededication of life with a very happy wife at his side. At the same time two of their sons also came to give their hearts to Christ. (That family has never been the same.)

The doctor shocked me when he said, "My wife and I have not had a vacation for thirteen years. I am a surgeon trained to make prompt decisions. While you were speaking, I decided we should take a vacation in the land of

Israel. We want you and your wife to go along as our guests and our guide."

He had no possible way of knowing that the Lord was answering my prayer in spectacular fashion. It had been two years since the Lord had called me from a relatively secure position of pastor and seminary teacher to the relatively insecure position of evangelist and Bible teacher, specializing in prophecy. In view of this new assignment, I knew I had to go back to Israel, but I did not know how that would be financially possible. My pictures and firsthand accounts from eight years before needed updating. Both the Lord and I knew another trip was necessary, but only one of us knew how it was going to happen.

That day during the blizzard, the Lord used this sermon to bring the doctor to Himself and me to the Holy Land. At the doctor's request we spent a whole month touring the Bible lands, especially Israel, in a limousine with a local guide. That cost two thousand dollars for me and two thousand dollars for my wife for a total of four thousand dollars. Things like that do not happen by accident. I call it a miracle.

Since that time the Lord has arranged to have me "guide" hundreds of Christians, Bibles in hand, through His land, the miracle land of Israel. And he has used this message in many places to bring many lost sinners to Himself and to bless untold thousands.

May all praise be to the God of Israel "who worketh all things after the counsel of his own will ... that we should be to the praise of his glory ...."

The Land of Miracles

It was ten o'clock at night. I was in a hotel on top of Mt. Carmel. You will remember Mt. Carmel as the place where Elijah called down fire from heaven to prove the existence of the true and living God.

Dr. Salstrand, my roommate for the night, was dressed for bed when he decided that he wanted to write a letter. Because he did not have any stationery, he asked me to go down to the lobby of the hotel to get some. I happened to be reading a book at the moment, and I wanted to finish it. But Dr. Salstrand insisted. He wouldn't take "no" for an answer, and I shall always be thankful that he did not.

In the lobby of the hotel I spoke to the man behind

Sunset over Mt. Carmel. *Matson Photo Service.*

the desk. It immediately became evident that he did not speak English, and I did not speak German. I understood what he was saying, but I did not know how to say "writing paper" in German. I'm a Pennsylvania Dutchman by birth, so I tried some Pennsylvania Dutch. That did not work. Then I thought of the German word "papier." His face lit up; I thought we had communicated.

He said, "Ja, ja," and reached under the desk and handed me a newspaper. Well, I guess that is what I had asked for, paper, but I did not know how to say "schreibes papier."

While we were having these linguistic difficulties, a young lady came into the lobby. In very good English, she said, "May I help you?" I explained the difficulty to her. "There isn't any in the desk," she said, "but I will get some for you." Whereupon, she left the lobby.

While she was gone, a friendly, elderly, rather heavy-set lady came strolling into the lobby. She took one look at me and recognized the fact that I was a foreigner. Then she walked up to me and started talking. Among other things, she wanted to know why I had come to the land of Israel. I told her that I had come to see a miracle. That took her by surprise, and she responded something like this: "This is the twentieth century, and we don't believe in miracles."

"Oh, but I do!" I exclaimed. "You have a lot of them here in this land."

About that time the young lady returned with the writing paper. As she approached us, the elderly lady introduced her by saying, "This is Mrs. So and So, the wife of the hotel manager, and I am Mrs. Ben Gurion, wife of the Prime Minister."

It was just as if you were downtown in one of the hotels of your city and happened to bump into Mrs. Nixon—just like that! The most important lady in the land of Israel, and there I was, talking to her. Of course, it took me by surprise, and I don't know exactly what happened in those few moments that followed.

When I got over the shock, I realized that she was inviting me to have tea with her. That frightened me a bit because I grew up on a farm in Lebanon County, Pennsylvania, and we never did specialize in Emily Post. I never learned how you cock that little finger just right when you sip tea with a Prime Minister's wife. I must admit I tried to talk her out of it, but I am glad to say that she wouldn't take "no" for an answer.

Now somebody here will lie awake tonight wondering whether my friend ever got his writing paper that night. The answer is, "No, he did not." He finally gave up and went to bed, wondering what in the world had happened to me.

Encounter With Mrs. Ben Gurion

Meanwhile, I was enjoying a wonderful time talking with the two women there in the lobby of the hotel on the top of Mt. Carmel. We were totally undisturbed except for one man who, from time to time, came strolling through the lobby, casting suspicious glances at me. The first time he went through, Mrs. Ben Gurion said, "That's my bodyguard; I get so sick and tired of him." So I tried to smile and look very friendly whenever he appeared.

During the first half hour, we had a delightful conversation. It was most interesting indeed! But all the while I was talking to the Lord, and I am so glad that our God does not go to bed early. I sent an SOS to heaven and found the "hot line" open. The Bible tells us that the Lord neither slumbers nor sleeps. His ear is always open to the prayers of His children. Expressed in words, my prayer would have been something like this: "Lord, this is a tremendous opportunity. Here is Mrs. Ben Gurion, wife of Israel's Prime Minister. Direct the conversation so I can give her the gospel."

Then I waited while she talked. She told me all about

The modern city of Tel Aviv, adjacent to the ancient city of Joppa, where Peter stayed by the shore with Simon a tanner. *Photo by Homer A. Kent, Jr.*

her wonderful husband. It seemed to me that she thought he was the greatest man in the world. (As far as a statesman is concerned, David Ben Gurion, I think, ranks near the top.) She had been born in New York City when Tel Aviv, now the largest city in Israel, was nothing but desert sand. Her husband had been a refugee from Eastern Europe and had come to this land with one burning dream—to re-establish and rebuild the State of Israel.

She talked for about half an hour when suddenly she said, "But what about you? I've been doing all the talking. Tell me about yourself." When she discovered that I was from a seminary in the States, something seemed to click in her mind. Grace Theological Seminary, Winona Lake, Indiana, meant nothing to her, but the word "seminary" did.

She said, "Well, then, you can tell me something I've been wanting to know. If Jesus was as powerful as they say He was, why did He die?" I hadn't said anything about Jesus. Suddenly she was asking me to tell her what I was wishing to tell her. And you realize, don't you, what a wonderful question she asked: "If Jesus was as powerful as they say He was, why did He die?"

I said, "Mrs. Ben Gurion, I would be delighted to give you the answer. Will you permit me to begin in the beginning?"

She said, "Yes, please do."

In the meantime I breathed another prayer. "Thank you, Lord. Now put the words into my mouth." I did not know exactly what I was going to say, but I started.

"Mrs. Ben Gurion," I said, "Your Scriptures (we call it the Old Testament) tell the story of how God, the Almighty Creator, made two perfect people and placed them in a beautiful garden, in a perfect environment. Because He was a God of love, a personal Being who desired love and fellowship, He made these lovely creatures. And he walked and talked with them, and they had a wonderful time together.

"But He warned them that they must never, under any circumstances, disobey Him. He was the omnipotent eternal God, and He could not possibly tolerate disobedience on the part of His subjects. That would be treason in God's empire; He called it 'sin.'

"But," I continued, "as you know, Mrs. Ben Gurion, Adam and Eve did exactly what God told them not to do. And the moment they disobeyed Him, physical death set in; for in that moment, the cells of their bodies began to die faster than the body could replace them. Physical death now was their portion. It was only a matter of time. In addition, spiritual death, which is separation from God, was an instant experience. Now the fellowship they had enjoyed so much was broken; they had sinned against God and the penalty for sin was death—separation. He was the very essence of holiness; they were sinners. Holiness and sin can know no fellowship. So what could God do?"

Impatiently she leaned forward in her chair as she exclaimed, "Yes! Yes! What did He do?"

I explained, "God devised a plan whereby these two need not perish. They could fellowship with God, and yet God could remain a perfect and holy God. He could not say, 'Well, I forgive you this time, but don't let it happen again.' An earthly judge could do so, but God couldn't. Therefore, His decree had to stand. Thus, He devised a plan that called for the sending of a substitute (one upon whom the death penalty did not rest) to come and take that death penalty in the place of and in the stead of the guilty ones. He would be the Redeemer, the Messiah.

"Mrs. Ben Gurion, right there in the book of Genesis, we have the first announcement of His coming. It is said one would come who would be the seed of a woman—this requires a virgin birth. All human beings are born as the seed of a man and a woman; but this man was to be unique. He would be born as the seed of a woman—a virgin birth. It was prophesied right there in Genesis, and it was said that eventually the day would come when He would crush the serpent's head. And all through your Scriptures, Mrs. Ben Gurion, we have the story of how God the Father revealed what He was going to do. One would come who would be called 'Shiloh.' He would be out of the tribe of Judah. He would be out of the family of Jesse. He would be heir to David's throne. But He would be led to the slaughter as a sheep, dumb before its shearer. Many prophecies were uttered about Him.

"As a matter of fact, there are more than thirty exact, precise prophecies uttered over a period of hundreds of years by many different authors, all of which were fulfilled in the life of one man in twenty-four hours. That man was Jesus Christ, and the twenty-four hour period was the day He died."

I was looking straight into her eyes as I said it. I wanted to see her reaction. She wanted to hear more, so I continued the story of redemption.

I wish I could tell you that Mrs. Ben Gurion accepted Christ as her Savior. I can only tell you that she said, "Mr. Meyer, you have a strong faith. My husband has a strong faith, too. Would you like to meet him?" She did not need to ask that question a second time.

So, in due time, I was to meet Mr. Ben Gurion, the first and, now former, Prime Minister of the State of Israel. But I will talk about that experience later when I deal with some of the prophecies involved in this subject.

FIRST MIRACLE

Preservation of the Jewish People

I talked to Mrs. Ben Gurion about an hour and a half. When I finished the explanation of the way of salvation, she said, "But what about the miracles?" So I told her about the miracle of fulfilled prophecy in relation to the Jews and the State of Israel.

And that is what I want to show you now.

So, if you will, please, open your Bibles, first of all, to a prophecy in the Book of Deuteronomy. Let's start in Chapter 28. Moses had come out of the land of Egypt with all the descendants of Jacob. They had been wandering through the wilderness forty years, and they were now about to enter the Promised Land. Moses, himself, would not be allowed to enter because of his disobedience to the Lord. He would walk up Mt. Pisgah to his own funeral, and there God would bury him, as you read in the end of the book of Deuteronomy. But just before his death, Moses stood there on the mountains of Moab, and turning to the Jewish people, he gave them his final instructions before he said goodbye to them. And as he stood there, he looked all over the Promised Land.

Standing on the mountains of Moab today, one can

Reclaimed farmland at the southern tip of the Sea of Galilee — Jordan Valley. *Matson Photo Service.*

look into the valley below and see the Dead Sea, fifty miles long and the lowest spot on earth. The water is so salty that not a living thing can exist in it. You can look away to the north on a clear day and see faintly the outline of the Sea of Galilee. And you can see the Jordan River, winding back and forth like a snake, as it flows down into the Dead Sea. You can look across the Dead Sea to the west and see the barren, desolate wilderness of Judea.

But it was not barren when Moses looked at it. In that day it was a land that "flowed with milk and honey"; it was a productive, fertile land. But because of their sins the Jews were driven out of the land, and it became desolate.

Off in the distance also to the west, one can see a hill at the top of the horizon. One can recognize it as that sacred spot from which the feet of Jesus last left this earth, the Mount of Olives. And though you cannot see it, you know that just on the other side lies the Holy City, the city named after heaven itself, JERUSALEM. And then you look away to the northwest, and you can see the hills of Samaria. And still farther to the north you can see the hills of Galilee. There it is! The Promised Land!

Moses saw it and called it the land of milk and honey. There Moses stood overlooking the Promised Land. Then he turned to the children of Israel, and gave them his final instructions. Follow in your Bible in Deuteronomy 28:1-2.

> And it shall come to pass, if thou shalt hearken diligently unto the voice of the Lord thy God, to observe and to do all his commandments which I command thee this day, that the Lord thy God will set thee on high above all nations of the earth; *And all these blessings* shall come on thee, and overtake thee, *if* thou shalt hearken unto the voice of the Lord thy God.

You ought to mark "all these blessings" in your Bible and then also mark the word "if." *All these blessings if* thou shalt hearken unto the voice of the Lord thy God! And in the verses to follow he enumerates many of the blessings that will be theirs if they are true and faithful and loyal and obedient to the Lord Jehovah after they have entered into the land.

But there is an alternative and we have it in verse 15:

> But it shall come to pass, if thou wilt not (now here

you ought to mark the words *'if'* and *'not'*) hearken unto the voice of the Lord thy God, to observe to do all his commandments and his statutes which I command thee this day; *that all these curses* shall come upon thee ...

Now mark that phrase, and you have the message. On the one hand, all these blessings *if;* on the other hand, all these curses *if not.* If they were true and faithful and loyal and obedient in their worship of the Lord Jehovah, and Him alone, God would bless them so that no power on earth could drive them out. He would give them military protection. In addition, he would control the elements so they would have material prosperity. Fields and

Arab shepherd with his sheep – olive trees in the background. *Matson Photo Service.*

flocks would flourish. They would have an abundance of food, shelter, and clothing. They would have plenty of everything, and they would be safe from their enemies. God promised material prosperity and military protection in exchange for loyal, loving, faithful obedience to Him. This is not the promise to the church. This is the promise to God's chosen earthly people—the Jews, or technically, the "Israelites."

On the other hand, if they would not faithfully serve and obey Him, then *all these curses* would come upon them; and in the verses to follow, God spells out all the problems and trials and tribulations and difficulties and sufferings that they would endure if they drifted away from the Lord Jehovah.

Moses, by divine inspiration, knew that eventually God would have to deal with these stubborn, rebellious, and stiff-necked people because he knew that even though they would serve Him spasmodically, in the final outcome they would be found worshiping idols like the Canaanites. Thus Moses uttered this tremendous prophecy found in Deuteronomy 28:64. It is the first of two great prophecies that I want you to observe. Mark verse 64 very carefully. It was uttered approximately 3500 years ago while the Israelites were on the mountains of Moab, overlooking the Promised Land. Notice carefully, they were not yet in the land, but here is the prophecy of their dispersion. Verse 64: "And the Lord shall scatter thee among all people, from the one end of the earth even unto the other . . . ."

That's it! Moses said it, and a thousand years later it was fulfilled. Actually it did not take that long for the northern kingdom to go off into captivity. As you know, under the sons of Solomon, the kingdom was divided. And the northern kingdom with its capital on the hill of Samaria was called Israel. The southern kingdom with its capital at Jerusalem was called Judah.

Over the centuries God pleaded with His people. He

tried desperately to keep them for Himself and to nurture them in loyalty and faithfulness. He raised up godly kings, priests, prophets, and judges from time to time. Occasionally, they would have a brief revival, but it did not last. Wicked rulers such as Jezebel and Ahab led the people away into the awful sins of the Canaanites which involved the burning of babies as they worshiped the devil. So it was that God finally could stand it no longer. He brought in the armies of Assyria to take the northern kingdom into captivity. Later He brought in the armies of Babylon from the east, and they took the southern kingdom. In round numbers we can say that a thousand years after Moses prophesied, the prophecy was fulfilled. Let me read it once more: Deuteronomy 28, verse 64: "And the Lord shall scatter thee among all people, from the one end of the earth even unto the other . . . ."

Now let us skip across the centuries to the middle of your Bible to the prophecies of Ezekiel. In chapter 36, we find the young prophet, Ezekiel, in the land of Babylon, the land of bondage. His people are not in the Promised Land now. Here in the land of captivity God brings Ezekiel upon the scene; and by divine instruction and inspiration, He proceeds to inform the people concerning the reason why they are now slaves in a foreign land instead of being in their own land—the land of blessing. Ezekiel looks across the span of future years and without indicating the time element, predicts the day will come when these dispersed Jews, scattered to the ends of the earth, will return to their homeland. He gives us one of the great prophecies of the Bible concerning the return of the Jewish people to the land of Israel, and you and I have lived to see it happen.

Let's look at the reason and then the prophecy. Turn to Ezekiel 36:16-18:

> Moreover the word of the Lord came unto me, saying, Son of man, when the house of Israel dwelt in their own land, they defiled it by their own way and

by their doings: their way was before me as the uncleanness of a removed woman. Wherefore I poured my fury upon them for the blood that they had shed upon the land, and for their idols wherewith they had polluted it.

The two key words are "blood" and "idols." You should underscore those words in your Bible.

For an explanation from the Bible itself so you will not depend upon private interpretation, turn to Jeremiah 19, verses 4 and 5. It might be well to mark this in your margin for ready reference. These verses spell out the exact reason for the dispersion of the Jews; there is no question about it. Ezekiel says that God was furious because His people did something that involved blood and idols. It made God so angry that He drove them out of the land. In essence, this is what we have read.

Now Jeremiah 19:4-5 tells us what is involved:

Because they have forsaken me, and have estranged this place, and have burned incense in it unto other gods, whom neither they nor their fathers have known, nor the kings of Judah, and have filled this place with the blood of innocents . . .

It says they burned incense in it unto other gods; this is idolatry. Verse 5 tells us plainly what the blood of innocents is: "They have built also the high places of Baal, to burn their sons with fire for burnt offerings unto Baal . . . ."

Imagine that! God's chosen earthly people had stooped so low in the sins of the Canaanites that in the worship of the idol Baal, which is a form of devil worship, they had actually brought their sweet, little, heaven-sent innocent babies and had burned them on the altar of the devil as they worshiped Lucifer. God in his heaven was furious! No wonder! A holy, righteous God had brought them out of the land of Egypt. By miracle after miracle He had led them through the Red Sea and through the wilderness

A view of Samaria from the Shechem Road. *Matson Photo Service.*

wanderings. He made their enemies fall before them as they entered the Promised Land. He had promised them prosperity and protection—everything they needed—if only they would be loyal and faithful. And here they were, worshiping like the Canaanites in the groves, engaging in immorality between men and women as part of the worship service, bringing their offspring and burning them as sacrifices upon the altar of the devil.

God in His heaven could not stand it. In a measure at least, I think we can understand God's fury.

Now turn to Ezekiel 36:19.

> And I (God is speaking) scattered them among the heathen. (And the word heathen is the word Gentiles. I will read it that way hereafter.) I scattered them among the Gentiles, and they were dispersed through the countries: according to their way and according to their doings I judged them. (God is speaking and telling the Jews why they are slaves in a foreign land.)
>
> Verse 20: And when they entered unto the Gentiles whither they went, they profaned my holy name (They dragged my name in the mud; that is what God is saying.), when they said to them, These are the people of the Lord, and are gone forth out of his land.

You see how it brought reproach upon the name of Jehovah. They claimed Jehovah as their God. But the pagans said, "Well, your God isn't strong enough to keep you and protect you, so here you are slaves. Your God must not be any good." God is telling the Jews that they dragged His name in the mud because of the awful things they did. Nevertheless, He preserved them in exile so that in due time He might return them to their land.

SECOND MIRACLE

Restoration of the Jewish People

Ezekiel rehearsed what had happened in the past, telling them why they were where they were, and then God looked across the years to announce what a glorious future they would have. He might have said, "I am finished with you. I will let you go the way of the people of other nations." But no, they were God's chosen earthly people. They bore His name. And because they bore His name, he was yet going to do a mighty work in them and through them. Don't forget, too, these were the people through whom Messiah would come.

Now Ezekiel tells us what God is going to do in verses 21-23:

> But I had pity for mine holy name, which the house of Israel had profaned among the Gentiles, whither they went. Therefore say unto the house of Israel, Thus saith the Lord God: I do not this for your sakes, (Notice that God is telling them they do not deserve what He is going to do.) O house of Israel, but for mine holy name's sake, which ye have profaned among the Gentiles, whither ye went. And I will sanctify my great name, which was profaned among the Gentiles, which ye have profaned in the midst of them; and the Gentiles shall know that I am the Lord, saith the Lord God, when I shall be sanctified in you before their eyes.

Verse 24 is the great prophecy. Please mark it distinctly in your Bible so you can see it immediately. It is a tremendous prophecy, having had its fulfillment in the lifetime of most individuals today. It was uttered twenty-five centuries ago, a thousand years after Moses spoke on the mountains of Moab: "For I will take you from among the Gentiles, and gather you out of all countries, and will bring you into your own land."

God has kept His word. That prophecy has been fulfilled literally. But before I rehearse the account of history, telling how that prophecy has been fulfilled in my lifetime, I want to show you another specific prophecy, in Chapter 37, verse 12 and verse 22.

THIRD MIRACLE

Resurrection of a Dead Nation

Here we have a precise, exact prophecy, giving the name the country would have when they returned. Remember when they left, they were two countries: Israel in the north, Judah in the south. And they went into captivity at different times to different places. God said that when they came back, there would be no more two nations upon the mountains of Israel. He told them there would be one country and the name of that country would be ISRAEL . . . I-S-R-A-E-L.

Now that is exactly what has happened. I will briefly give you the story of Ezekiel's valley of the dry bones (Ezekiel 37:1-12). I presume you have heard the Negro spiritual: "The foot bone connected to the ankle bone; the ankle bone connected to the shin bone; the shin bone connected to the knee bone; the knee bone connected to the thigh bone; the thigh bone connected to the hip bone, ..." That story comes from this passage where Ezekiel looked out over a valley, and God said, "What do you see?"

Ezekiel said, "I see a valley full of dry bones."

God proceeded to tell him, "This is the whole house of Israel." They were not in a cemetery but scattered in the graveyard of the nations, all over the world.

And the bones said, "Our hope is cut off, we are lost! We are away from our homeland. We have no flag, no king, no country, and there is no hope for us."

But God said, "Prophesy to these dry bones and speak in the name of the Lord." And Ezekiel says, "So I prophesied." Verses 11 and 12:

> Then he said unto me, Son of man, these bones are the whole house of Israel: behold, they say, Our bones are dried, and our hope is lost: we are cut off for our parts. Therefore prophesy and say unto them, Thus saith the Lord God; Behold, O my people (No-

The hills of Israel and a watchtower in the vineyard. *Levant Photo Service.*

tice that it is addressed to the Jewish people.), I will open your graves (Remember, that is the graveyard of the nations; no one talks in a cemetery.), and cause you to come up out of your graves and bring you into the land of (Canaan? No! Palestine? No! Philistia? No! Any one of the ancient names of that land might have been used, but God said it would be)—"ISRAEL."

That is exactly the way the prophecy was fulfilled. Let me explain.

For approximately 2500 years this prophecy lay dormant; many individuals thought that God was finished with the Jew, that this prophecy would never be literally fulfilled. Even a few years back there were preachers who were saying that God was certainly not going to fulfill this prophecy literally; but God has a way of fulfilling His word—not only to the word, but also to the very letter.

Remember, Jesus said every "jot" and every "tittle" must be fulfilled. A jot is the smallest letter in the Hebrew alphabet which is the language that was used when the Old Testament was written. It is like a comma only it is a little higher. The tittle is part of a letter. When two letters are almost alike, such as "n" and "m", the difference between them is a tittle. I am trying to impress upon you that God fulfills prophecy with divine precision. He fulfills it to the very letter and even to the half letter. What a God! What a book!

The twentieth century has witnessed an explosion of fulfilled prophecy, and this is one of the most dramatic and spectacular of all. In 1897 Theodore Hertzl, at the head of World Jewry, conducted a conference in which he predicted that within fifty years the nation of Israel would again be in existence. He died just before it happened, and he missed the prophecy by one year, but it did happen! The nation of Israel was "born in a day."

Remember Moses had said that wherever they went on this earth there would be no peace and no rest under the soles of their feet. In the morning they would say, "If only it were evening." In the evening they would say, "If only it were morning." And wherever they would go, there would be persecution, trouble, and difficulty. And that is exactly the way it happened.

In the twentieth century they began to return from various countries to their ancient homeland in sufficient numbers to fulfill the prophecy.

But they had a difficult time. Just north of the Sea of Galilee is a valley in which your Bible maps show Lake Huleh. There was never a really good lake there; it was just a mosquito-infested swamp. Many of the people died from malaria as they tried to farm the swamplands of this valley. But the Jews have now drained it, and today it is beautiful, rich, fertile farmland.

The hills of Israel were barren, desolate, and rocky. But the Jews continued to come. Following the first World War, the Balfour Declaration issued by the British government favored the establishment of a Jewish "National Home" in Palestine. The League of Nations, followed by the United Nations, gave Britain the "mandate" to furnish a government for the land of Palestine and to provide a homeland for the Jews. Britain carried out the mandate for nearly three decades.

Meanwhile a paperhanger from Germany by the name of Schickelgruber rose to power under the name of Adolph Hitler. He boasted the Third Reich would last a thousand years. But he made a fatal mistake, and the Third Reich went down to a flaming death in a little more than a decade. Adolph Hitler gave the order, and six million of God's chosen earthly people were butchered and murdered in the most barbaric fashion that the mind of man, influenced by Satan, could concoct. You can walk into the museum in Jerusalem today and see cakes of soap made by Hitler's henchmen from the flesh of Jews. It was a Jewish holocaust, inhuman and beastly.

Then we remember how God said to Abraham, "Those

Early Jewish immigrants "reclaiming the wastelands." *Matson Photo Service.*

that bless you, I will bless, those that curse you, I will curse." Adolph Hitler and his Nazi Germany cursed the Jew, and Germany went down to utter defeat.

Then the Jews had a fresh motive for going home, and they began to return in ever-increasing numbers to their ancient homeland. Boat loads, crammed to the rails with Jewish immigrants, sailed to Palestine.

In the meantime, the Grand Mufti of Jerusalem, the religious head of all Moslem Arabs who was pro-Nazi during the war, began to incite the Arabs against the Jews. They had been living peacefully together, but the Arabs then began to conduct raids on the Jewish villages and vice versa. It became quite intolerable and the British were in the very middle of it. They were trying to keep peace; but to please the Arabs, they began to restrict

Jewish immigration.

A boat crowded to overflowing with refugees from Europe was refused immediate permission to dock. The British, in trying to decide what to do, waited too long. The boat sank and every last person on board was drowned. The Jews were infuriated; and from then on, they began to fight the British.

The Arabs were fighting the British because they were letting Jews come in. The Jews were fighting the British because there were too many delays and restrictions. The Jews even blew up one wing of their pride and joy, the King David Hotel in Jerusalem, because it was headquarters for the British. It became intolerable! The British could not stand it any longer. They said, "We are quitting." They announced that at midnight, following the fourteenth day of May, 1948, they would vacate the mandate and would leave the country. Thus, the British Empire abandoned Palestine and the Middle East.

On the afternoon of May 14, 1948, David Ben Gurion, a former refugee from Europe, stood before a packed auditorium in Tel Aviv. At precisely four o'clock he read a document which ended with words that were to make Bible-believing Christians all over the world shout, "Hallelujah, God is on the throne." That document ended with these historic words, "I now declare to be in existence the State of *Israel!*" The crowd burst into weeping unashamedly. For this they had waited and hoped and prayed for two and a half millenia. Now, at last, it had happened!

At midnight on May 14 (the beginning of the 15th) the flag of ancient Israel, the Star of David, was hoisted in the Middle East. Israel, a dead nation for almost 2500 years, was again in existence.

Incidentally, at that time the man who was President of the United States was expecting to run again, but everybody said he could not possibly win. It was a foregone conclusion that he would lose to Tom Dewey. However, eleven minutes after Israel declared its independence, he announced to the world that the United States recognized the State of Israel. I think that event made all the difference in the election of Harry S. Truman. I think that is the reason why he won the next election to everybody's surprise. God blesses those who bless His people. He curses those who curse them (Genesis 12:3).

Be that as it may, the following day it was announced to the world that Israel was again in existence. The Star of David was hoisted in the Holy Land. The flag of Israel was flying. The headlines blared out the news. Christians were excited. The prophecy of Ezekiel, dormant for twenty-five centuries, had leaped to fulfillment. God had done a mighty thing! Here something happened that had never happened before in the history of nations. I challenge you to find a precedent. There is nothing like it in all history!

I was explaining this miracle to Mrs. Ben Gurion when she said, "Oh, but my husband did that."

To be sure, she had a great husband and he had a lot to do with it, under God. But I said, "Mrs. Ben Gurion, my mother's grandfather came from Germany to America, married, and had a large family. My mother and her brothers and sisters were never called Germans; they were Americans. It took only one generation for them to lose their identity of national origin. That is the law of science, the law of sociology. That is the law of rhyme and reason, but that is not the way of the Jew."

The Jew left his homeland and went to Assyria and to Babylon. From there he went to the ends of the earth, to every continent, and to the isles of the sea. But wherever he went, he remained a Jew—not for a generation or two or ten, not for a hundred years nor a thousand, but for 2500 years. God seems deliberately to have allowed enough time to pass so that fulfillment of the prophecy would require a miracle.

Then it was as if God suddenly said, "Now it is time to

Jerusalem viewed from the slope of the Mount of Olives. *Levant Photo Service.*

go home"; and with the dawn of the twentieth century, they began to come from all directions of the globe. They came from more than a hundred countries of the world, talking dozens of different languages. They represented many different cultures and modes of living. But they were Jews returning to their tiny homeland to work out a culture and establish a nation where they could live in decency, dignity, and independence.

It was a difficult situation, it still is today. They had an overabundance of doctors and lawyers and professional men. You know that the Jews in this country are not farmers; they are professional men. What they needed were farmers to raise food, men to dig irrigation ditches, carpenters to build homes, etc. So that is what these men did. And whatever the men did, the women also did, including soldiering.

FOURTH MIRACLE

Preservation of the New Nation

Now, notice the miracles involved. First, we have the miracle of the preservation of these people in exile. Secondly, we have the miracle of the restoration of these scattered people to their ancient homeland. Thirdly, we have the miracle of the resurrection of a dead nation. Then we have the miracle of the preservation of that nation after it came into existence. Let me tell you about that.

Within twenty-four hours after David Ben Gurion said, "I now declare to be in existence the State of Israel," he had upon his shoulders more problems and responsibilities than any human ruler has ever had in so short a time. Before this brand new nation had time to organize all of the ministries, services, and offices of government, it was invaded by five hostile armies with more to come later. From every side there was an approaching army on the march. The only friendly shore was the Mediterranean,

One of the reforested areas in Israel. *Levant Photo Service.*

and the Arab governments announced on their radios, "We will drown every Jew in the sea."

The military odds were overwhelming. The Jews were outnumbered more than forty to one. And yet they did not lose! There is no adequate explanation apart from the word "miracle." It was something which only God could do.

God said He would bring them back and put them on the mountains of Israel. And He did it. He also said, "Behold, I am for you." And that, my friends, made all the difference in the world in 1948, and it made all the difference in the world in the Six Day War in 1967.

But now let us read Ezekiel 36:8: "But ye, O mountains of Israel, ye shall shoot forth your branches, and yield your fruit to my people of Israel; for they are at hand to come."

The story of the trees is a fascinating one. On the Arab side of the line, the hills are mostly barren and desolate; but on the Jewish side, they have planted more than a hundred million trees. First, they were little seedlings a few inches high; then they were a few feet high; then, as high as a church; and finally, mature forests. This you find all over the hills of Israel, but especially around Jerusalem.

God said 2500 years ago in the context that spoke of the return of His people that when they came home, He would say to the mountains of—not Jordan, not Iraq, not Syria or Egypt, but—Israel, "Shoot forth your branches, my people are home." I saw it! It is true! God keeps His word and that to the very letter! The trees are growing!

Now look what God says in Ezekiel 36:9-12:

> For, behold, I am for you, and I will turn unto you, (and that makes all the difference in the world: God is on their side) and ye shall be tilled and sown; And I will multiply men upon you, all the house of Israel, even all of it (There never were ten lost tribes with God; God has them all in control; they are all involved in this; so let God worry about the tribes.): and the cities shall be inhabited, and the wastes shall be builded: And I will multiply upon you man and beast; and they shall increase and bring fruit: and I will settle you after your old estates, and will do better unto you than at your beginnings: and ye shall know that I am the Lord. Yea, I will cause men to walk upon you, even my people Israel; and they shall possess thee, and thou shalt be their inheritance, and thou shalt *no more* henceforth bereave them of men.

It is my opinion that the prophecies indicate the Jews will never again be driven out of their land, except when they flee to Petra during the second half of the Tribulation Period (Revelation 12).

It was my privilege to say to Mr. Ben Gurion, the Prime Minister upon our meeting, "Are you aware of the fact that you, the Jews, are in the land as the result of fulfilled Bible prophecy?"

He smiled knowingly and said, "Yes, we know that."

An area of complete reforestation, Jerusalem Corridor, Israel. *Levant Photo Service.*

Israel's first Prime Minister, David Ben Gurion, and his wife, Mrs. Ben Gurion. They are shown shortly after their retirement from public life, in the doorway of their home in Sdeh Boker, a tiny village south of Biblical Beersheba. *United Press photo.*

The next question was, "Do you realize that you will have much more land in due time than you have now?"

He smiled again and said, "Yes, we know that, too!"

I said, "Are you aware of the fact that the day is coming soon when Israel will be the leading nation of the world?"

He answered quickly, "Oh, no, that is not in the Bible." He said, "I have read the Old Testament in Hebrew, of course, and I have read the New Testament in Greek." Then I remembered that Mrs. Ben Gurion had told me that he had taught himself five languages, one of them being English and one of them, Greek. He read the New

Testament in its original language, Greek. Imagine that!

Well, he read a little too fast. It is there. In Deuteronomy 28:13 Moses said Israel would be the head and not the tail. Indeed, in due time, Israel is going to be the leading nation of the world.

When he was asked what he thought of Messiah, he said, "Messiah is an ideal, not a person." I was sad to hear it. An ideal, not a person? Messiah, to him, was the State of Israel: Zionism. That is, the effort of men to establish a Jewish homeland.

But I was thrilled a few years later when I walked down the street of Jerusalem and picked up an English copy of the Jerusalem *Post* and read the headlines. It said that the Prime Minister had addressed scholars from all over the world who were meeting in Jerusalem for special study. He had welcomed them, officially, as Prime Minister of the land. Then he said, "Now, speaking as a layman, I want to suggest that you put on the agenda for study the Messianic vision in relation to the redemption of our people and all the peoples of the world, which is after all, the soul of Judaism."

My heart skipped a beat. I almost shouted "Hallelujah" walking down the street of Jerusalem. Mr. Ben Gurion, the Prime Minister, was asking the scholars of the world to study the very thing I had spent an hour and a half explaining to his wife some years before. The Messianic vision is the story of how God is going to send Messiah to save His people: the story that prevails all through the Old Testament. Mr. Ben Gurion was asking scholars of the world to study this!

He is an old man now, but he knows the gospel. Whether or not he has accepted it secretly, I do not know, but he is very friendly to the Christians. Incidentally, Mrs. Ben Gurion passed away several years ago.

FIFTH MIRACLE
Resurrection of a Dead Language

Mr. Ben Gurion has done a great work in that land in numerous ways. In the first place, God used him to establish the nation (as first Prime Minister). In addition, he was responsible, undoubtedly, more than any other individual for bringing about the Hebrew language as a living language after all these years of its being a dead language.

Hebrew is the language of the government. It is the language of the newspapers. It is the language of the street, and it is the language of the schools. The classes in the University of Jerusalem are taught in Hebrew.

SIXTH MIRACLE
Restoration of Jerusalem to the Jews

Briefly, we have one more miracle which is highly significant and important. It is the Jewish domination of Jerusalem after the Gentile rule of nineteen centuries.

Somewhere around June 4, 1967, a Jewish lady phoned my dear friend, Dr. Dennison, a dentist in the city of Columbus, Ohio. He is a very gracious and witnessing Christian. In tears, she said, "Dr. Dennison, what am I going to do? I just read the papers. Nasser is going to wipe out Israel. My brothers and sisters and my relatives are all going to be killed." She wept as she said again, "What am I going to do?"

Dr. Dennison answered confidently as he assured her, "Don't worry. Israel cannot lose." Three days later, the papers related that Israel had won the most smashing victory against the most overwhelming odds in all military history. This Jewish lady then inquired, "Dr. Dennison, how did you know?"

He answered, "It is all in the Bible."

In Luke 21:24, Jesus said Jerusalem would be trodden

Orthodox Jew praying at the Western Wall in Jerusalem.

down by the Gentiles until the times of the Gentiles be fulfilled. Since A.D. 70, when Jerusalem was destroyed by the Romans, there has not been one day when the Jews have held dominion over that city. But on June 6, 1967, they overran the city and that prophecy was fulfilled as the Jews crashed through the Mandelbaum Gate and took the old city of Jerusalem.

For the first time in 2500 years, there is no nation over them; no one can tell them what they must do. The Jews, with the help of God, did this by themselves; but some of them do not recognize God's part. They have knocked down the partition wall, removed the Mandelbaum Gate and the barbed wire fences so that Jerusalem is no longer a divided city. They have cleared away the old houses around the Western Wall to make room for the crowds of worshipers who come to pray. The old city is once again in Jewish hands. Moshe Dayan says, "We will never give it up."

One can now walk down the streets of Old Jerusalem, and he can find Jews and Arabs walking side by side where no Jew was seen from 1948 to 1967.

Nineteen centuries ago Jesus foretold events that could not have been fulfilled without the element of the supernatural. Yet these events have taken place exactly as foretold—all in my lifetime! What an exciting day to be alive! We are living in the end time of the Gentile age and that means JESUS IS COMING SOON!

Restatement of the Miracles

Thirty-five hundred years ago (Deuteronomy 28:64), Moses foretold the dispersion of the Jewish people even before they were in the land. Roughly, a thousand years later, his prophecy was completely fulfilled.

Twenty-five hundred years ago, God raised up the prophet, Ezekiel, in the land of captivity in Babylon to tell the Jewish people that it was because of their awful

A Yemenite Jew in the city of Tel Aviv. *Levant Photo Service.*

sins that they were slaves in a foreign land instead of free people in their own land of blessing. Then Ezekiel went on to foretell their future. He told them that one day God would bring them back to their own land and that it would be called "Israel" (Ezekiel 36 and 37). Now, after all these centuries of time, God has fulfilled His word. Prophecy has become history in every detail.

Nearly two thousand years ago Jesus foretold the utter destruction of Jerusalem which happened about thirty-seven years later. And then He said Jerusalem would be under Gentile rule until the end of the age. We are now at that point in history where this, too, has been literally fulfilled against all rational, logical or reasonable possibilities.

To accomplish all this, God performed miracle after miracle. Let me repeat them for you.

1. The *preservation of the Jewish people in exile* for 2500 years even though they were scattered all over the world.

2. The *restoration of these people to their land* which to them is home even though they had been gone for so long.

3. The *resurrection of a dead nation,* Israel, announcing exactly to the letter what the name of that nation would be.

4. The *preservation of that brand new nation,* population slightly over two million people, even though one hundred and ten million of the enemy completely surrounded them and fanatically insisted on their annihilation.

5. The *resurrection of a dead language,* Hebrew, the language of the Old Testament.

6. The *restoration of Jerusalem to Jewish domination* after nearly two thousand years of Gentile rule.

And there you have it, my friends, the story of the Miracle of Israel. One must be intellectually and spiritu-

Aerial view of Jerusalem showing the temple area. *Matson Photo Service.*

ally blind if he cannot see the God of prophecy unfolding His plans and purposes in the history of our time.

Personal Preparation

All of this is so very important because it means the end of the age is near. Jesus is coming again. The great question remains: Are you ready?

If you are ready, you can say with John, "... Amen. Even so, come, Lord Jesus" (Revelation 22:20).

But if you are not ready, then the whole purpose of this message is to tell you how to prepare yourself.

You cannot buy your way to heaven by purchasing a ticket. There isn't enough money in the whole world to buy one. Jesus said it is easier to put a camel through the eye of a needle than for a rich man to go to heaven. So money is not the answer (Matthew 19:24).

You cannot earn your way to heaven by being good because the Bible says, "There is none righteous, no, not one.... For all have sinned, and come short of the glory of God" (Romans 3:10, 23).

You cannot work your way to heaven because the Bible says that all our righteousnesses are as filthy rags in God's sight (Isaiah 64:6).

You cannot beg your way to heaven because the Bible says that in that day some will plead, "Lord, Lord," but He will answer, "Depart from me, ye workers of iniquity. I never knew you!" (Luke 13:25-27 and Matthew 8:22-23).

You cannot gamble your way to heaven by saying, "I will take my chances." God is not running a lottery. He said, "The soul that sinneth, it shall die. . . . The wages of sin is death" (Ezekiel 18:4 and Romans 6:23).

You cannot hitchhike your way to heaven by riding on the good reputation of a godly mother, father, brother, sister, or friend. The Bible says that everyone must answer for himself (II Corinthians 5:10).

You cannot "learn" your way to heaven by making education your god. The Bible speaks of such in these words: ". . . Ever learning, and never able to come to the knowledge of *the truth.*" *The truth* is Christ. Education is not the answer (II Timothy 3:7 and John 14:6).

You cannot "hypocrite" your way to heaven by joining a church in the hope of somehow sliding by unnoticed when other members enter. The Bible says the man without a wedding garment will not be admitted to the wedding. ". . . God is not mocked: for whatsoever a man soweth, that shall he also reap" (Galatians 6:7).

No! No! No! None of these methods will ever get you through the pearly gates.

Jesus said in John 14:6, *"I* am the way, the truth, and the life; no man cometh unto the Father, but by me." Christ is the answer.

You see, we are all sinners in God's sight, hopelessly lost and doomed to eternal separation from a perfect, righteous, holy God, doomed to suffer in the fires of hell for all eternity. One thing is sure: The lost will suffer forever in hell. In Matthew 25:41, Jesus said, ". . . Depart from me, ye cursed, into everlasting fire, prepared for the devil and his angels." Oh, how awful and how final are His words in verse 46: "And these shall go away into everlasting punishment." That is why this whole business is so very, very serious. It involves the destiny of your soul for all eternity!

But praise God, there is a balm in Gilead to heal the sin-sick soul! "Christ died for our sins." Paul wrote this to the Corinthians (I Corinthians 15:3). You see, God is a God of love, and He is not willing that any should perish (II Peter 3:9). So He sent His Son to die in the sinner's place. Christ, in His death, took your sin upon Himself and paid the penalty so that the penalty need not be exacted from you. So we read: "He who knew no sin became sin for us that we might be made the righteousness of God in Him" (II Corinthians 5:21). "When we were yet sinners, Christ died for us" (Romans 5:8). That is the provision God has made for us.

Having thus paid the price, God offered salvation as a free gift to "whosoever will" (Revelation 22:17). This is also clearly stated in Romans 10:13, ". . . whosoever shall call upon the name of the Lord shall be saved."

When an individual, in simple, childlike, trusting faith, casts himself on the mercy of God by calling on God to forgive his sins in the name of Jesus, God always does His part. There is forgiveness that results in inner peace and joy heretofore unknown. (Philippians 4:7 and I Peter 1:8.)

There follows an assurance of salvation that makes one sing, "Jesus is the joy of living." Why don't you try it?

"For by grace are ye saved through faith; and that not of yourselves: it is the gift of God: Not of works, lest any man should boast" (Ephesians 2:8-9).

This is serious business! Don't put it off! You want to be ready when He comes? Then ask Christ to come into your heart right now as we bow our heads in prayer. Let us pray!

"Our heavenly Father, we praise thee for thy Word and thank Thee that it is not written in vague generalities so that we must guess and suppose and argue about its meaning. But we thank Thee that it is exact and precise. It is definite and final. Thus saith the Lord! We have seen these things come to fulfillment in our own lifetime, and now, O God, we thank thee for the evidence thou hast presented of the truth. Even though we accept by faith, thou has allowed us to see these wonderful things come to pass. And thus we have proof of the truth.

"Now we pray that every person may put his faith and trust in Christ. If there is anyone who has not publicly done so, then help him to do it now. Help him to pray the sinner's prayer and ask Christ to come into his heart and forgive his sins. Then, O God, write his name in the Lamb's book of life; make him one of thy dear children;

View of the Garden of Gethsemane on the slope of the Mount of Olives. *Matson Photo Service.*

give him the gift of eternal life as the Holy Spirit comes to dwell within him; wash him in the blood of the Lamb and make him whiter than snow!

"For those of us, Lord, who bear the name of Christ, help us to live for Jesus and cause us to get excited about the event that is coming, when we shall all be instant astronauts, when we shall sail away through space at the speed of thought in glorified heavenly bodies, forever to be with our Lord and forever to be like Him. May we thrill with the thought that it could happen today! And may we rejoice to know that it certainly is going to happen soon. So finish the message in every heart; accomplish thy purpose in each of us for our good and for thy glory. We pray it in the lovely name of Jesus. Amen."